Dedicated to children of all ages who know how it feels to lose a friend.

JCJ

To Anne…who, long ago, told her little sister that the secret to being a good artist is to just keep practicing.

HS

ACKNOWLEDGEMENTS

Sarah Gail Mook,
who died at age 8
on December 14, 1995

Brittany Elizabeth Pasqual
(lovingly known to all as "Brit")
who died at age 5 on July 1, 2001

and

The Publications Grant Committee
Philadelphia Yearly Meeting
of the
Religious Society of Friends

who are responsible for
the writing and publication of this book.

"*Strawberry Jam*" was written in 1996 and given to Sarah's schoolmates as they faced the loss of their friend. Years later, I had the honor of assisting at the memorial service for Brit. Her family donated the ISBN for this book in Brit's memory. Finally, last March, the PYM Grant Committee provided the basic funding for the illustrations and professional publication of *"I Hate Strawberry Jam."*

I am deeply grateful to two very special little girls, their loving families, the Philadelphia Yearly Meeting, Hillary Spitzer for being so wonderful to work with, and to my friends and family, especially my husband, Seymour, for their support and encouragement.

It is my sincerest hope that grieving children of all ages, races, and religions gain knowledge and comfort from this book.

Judith C. Joseph
August 2002

CHAPTER 1

I used to love strawberry jam! When other kids had peanut butter and jelly sandwiches, I had peanut butter and strawberry jam sandwiches. It was my very favorite food…until that summer.

It was a beautiful sunshiny day. School was over, Mom and I had just come home from swimming, and I was sitting at the kitchen table having one of my wonderful sandwiches. Mom doesn't like it when I play with my food, but when she wasn't looking I would squish the strawberries out of my sandwich and eat them whole. We'd had a great morning; I was going to ride my bike that afternoon, and I was about as happy as I could be!

My mom works for the Commonwealth of Pennsylvania but she was on vacation for the month of July. We'd been doing lots of fun things and had taken my best friend PJ along for some of them. When Mom went back to work in August, PJ and I were going to go to day camp for the first time. He and I were excited about all the new things that were happening that summer.

The phone rang and my mom answered it. I was glad she was busy because it meant I'd have more time to squish and eat the strawberries. Mom made a strange noise, hung up the phone, and was busy running water at the sink. After a few minutes, I realized that she was crying. I'd only seen my mom cry a few times before. It was usually when she was watching a real happy or a real sad movie on TV. I got out of my chair, went over to the sink and hugged her around the waist.

"What's the matter, Mom? Why are you crying?" She knelt down and hugged me.

"Oh honey, please let's go sit down. I have to talk to you." She took my hand, and we walked back to the table and sat down. Mom was holding my hand so tight it hurt. All of a sudden I felt scared and didn't know why.

"I have very sad news. That was PJ's mom on the phone. She knows that you're PJ's best friend," my mom was saying. "Mrs. Gonzales wanted to tell us what happened, before we heard it on the news or from someone else. PJ got hurt this morning. The doctors tried very hard to make him well again, but they couldn't."

"What do you mean the doctors couldn't make him well again?" I asked. "Why would PJ be on the news? Where is he? We're supposed to go bike riding this afternoon."

My mom looked at me with the saddest look I'd ever seen. "PJ was out in his backyard playing on the big, old, oak tree. He had a long rope, and was pretending he was Superman and that he could fly. Somehow he slipped and the rope got tangled around his neck. His mom saw him fall and ran out to help. She got him down, but he wasn't breathing. The rescue squad tried for a long time to get PJ breathing again, but they couldn't. PJ died a little while ago."

My stomach felt awful. I just couldn't understand. PJ dead? How could that be? He's only a kid like me. The only other person I'd ever known who died was our neighbor, old Mr. Levine. He used to always say "hi" to me and we'd sit on his front steps and talk. But he was *real* old.

I looked at my mom and said, "Children don't die, only sick, old people die."

Mom tried to explain that children sometimes *do* die. I started to cry and told her that she must have lied to me when old Mr. Levine died.

She had said then, "When people get old, their bodies can just wear out. Mr. Levine was worn out and tired. He'd lived a good life, and it was time for him to go."

Well, PJ wasn't old and worn out! How could he be dead? I wasn't even sure I knew what *dead* meant. When my goldfish died, we went to the pet store and got another one, but after Mr. Levine died, his house was empty for a long time. His grown-up children came to clean it, and then a man and woman with a little baby moved in. The new people never spoke to me when I passed the house. It made me sad that Mr. Levine wasn't there anymore. Did *dead* mean that PJ was gone, and would never come back?

My mom was trying to talk to me, but she was upset, too. She was trying to tell me, "Most of the time, children don't die. They live to grow up and have children of their own. Children only die when they are very, very sick or when there's been a terrible accident. PJ had an accident."

"An accident!" I argued. "How could he die in the big, old oak tree? We climb that tree all of the time." I was getting angry. "This is stupid. I'll bet he's only pretending, like we do when we play space warriors. He's good at playing dead, and I bet he's just got everyone fooled."

I was crying hard because I knew, down deep, that it wasn't pretend. Mom hugged me again and tried to make me feel better. "Why don't you take a few deep breaths and finish your sandwich. We can talk about this again later."

I did something really awful then. I got very angry and threw my sandwich on the floor. I shouted, "I don't want this old sandwich, I hate strawberry jam," and ran out of the kitchen door.

CHAPTER 2

I ran down the street toward PJ's house. I ran so hard it hurt. As I got to his house I saw that there were strange cars in the driveway, even a police car. I was all out of breath and didn't want to talk to anyone, so I went around to the backyard. There was no one there. PJ's baseball and bat were on the ground and his bike was behind the garage where he always left it. I couldn't believe that PJ was dead and never coming back. It couldn't be. I picked up PJ's bat and walked back to the old oak tree. I was still crying and angry. I swung the bat and just kept hitting the tree as hard as I could, over and over again.

I was so upset I didn't even hear the door of the house open. PJ's mother had seen me and came out into the yard. When I finally stopped hitting the tree, she put her hand on my shoulder. She was crying and said, "I saw him out here on the tree. I should have stopped him. Now, it's too late. I should have stopped him."

We hugged each other tight. "Mrs. Gonzales, we played on this big old tree all the time. It wasn't your fault. It was the stupid tree! Please don't cry."

PJ's mom looked at me, "I know you're right. It wasn't my fault. It wasn't the tree's fault either. I just wish we could start today over again, and keep the accident from ever happening."

My insides hurt as I saw how sad Mrs. Gonzales was. She told me that she needed to cry to let the sadness out. I didn't know what she meant because I was crying, and the sadness still felt stuck inside me. I wished like I had never wished before that it was all a dream. I was going to wake up and find PJ standing at the door of my room.

Just then my mom came around the side of the house. She gave Mrs. Gonzales a hug, "I'm so sorry about PJ. I'll bring dinner for you all later. If there is anything else we can do, just let us know."

PJ's mom looked down at me and said, "Please come and visit us often. You will always remind us of the fun and good times in PJ's life. He was so glad to have you for his friend."

The hurt inside me got bigger and all I could do was nod my head. My mom put her arm around me, said good-bye to Mrs. Gonzales, and we left.

We were both quiet all the way home. As we walked into the kitchen, I saw that my sandwich was still on the floor. I looked at my mom, "Mom, I don't even know why I threw the sandwich on the floor." She helped me clean it up and explained that sometimes, when people hear news that hurts them or makes them sad, they do things that don't make any sense. I understood. Throwing my sandwich on the floor made no sense at all, nothing did.

I went upstairs to my room and sat on the bed feeling very, very strange. Everything looked different, nothing seemed right. It's hard to explain how I felt. It was as if my whole body felt like my foot feels after I've sat on it too long.

CHAPTER 3

I must have fallen asleep because it was dark when I sat up. I could hear my mom and dad talking downstairs and I thought, "Was it just a very bad dream? Is PJ really dead?"

I went down and knew as soon as I saw my parents that it wasn't a dream. Mom still looked sad and my dad hugged me, "I'm so sorry about PJ. He was such a good friend. We'll all miss him."

Mom said she'd brought dinner to PJ's family while I was asleep. She asked me if I wanted something to eat. I didn't think I was hungry, but when she put the food in front of me, I did eat. I can't even remember what it was.

My dad sat with me at the table. He and Mom said there were some things we had to talk about. They told me that PJ's big brother, Don, had come home from college where he had a summer job. His sister, Maria, was home from 4H camp. Mr. and Mrs. Gonzales had spent the afternoon calling friends and family to tell them what had happened. They were all very sad and very tired.

I looked at my dad, "Why do people have to die? Why did old Mr. Levine and PJ have to die? At Quaker First Day School, the teachers say that God loves us and takes care of us. How can that be, if our friends have to die?"

My dad thought for a while. "Do you remember your last birthday? How excited you were when you saw all of the wrapped presents?" I nodded. "Well, was it the fancy packages you were excited about, or what was in them?"

I didn't know what packages had to do with dying, but I answered, "I wanted what was inside."

My mom sat down. "Most people believe that our body is just the 'box' we come in. It's only the body that dies.

Our spirit, the real *us*, is what's 'inside the package'. That spirit never dies; it stays alive in the hearts and minds of those who love us. We also believe that our spirit lives on with God, and is very, very happy."

"But that doesn't make me not miss PJ," I said.

"We know," answered Mom. "The hardest part of someone dying is how much *we* miss them. The 'missing' is what hurts so much. I promise you, it won't hurt this much forever. It never goes away completely, but you'll be able to remember PJ, and smile at all the fun you had together. It'll take some time for your bruised spirit to heal."

"My spirit, the *me* inside my package?" I asked. It was funny to think of my "spirit," but bruised was a very good way to describe how I felt inside.

Dad explained, "When someone dies, those who love them want to honor them, and say good-bye in a special way. Different people honor their dead in different ways. There is usually some sort of ceremony to remember and pray for the spirit of the dead person. The body, the empty package, is respectfully buried in a cemetery or it is burned and the ashes are taken to a special place. "

Both burying and burning sounded terrible to me. I had to think about that. My parents left me in the kitchen and told me to take my time. After a while I decided—if it's only the "package" that's burned or buried, and the spirit was free, I guess it's OK.

My head was all mixed up. I still couldn't believe that PJ was dead. Maybe his spirit *was* still alive. That didn't help me any. I couldn't see him, hear him, or play with him. I needed some more answers.

CHAPTER 4

I went into the living room and asked, "What kind of a special good-bye do people say?"

"There are many ways of saying good-bye," my dad answered. "A funeral or a memorial service are two ways. As Quakers, we have a memorial service after the body's been buried or burned. Friends come to the Meeting House to talk with God about the person who died, and then share wonderful, loving memories with each other. PJ's family is Catholic, and they do it a bit differently. There will be a ceremony called a "Funeral Mass" in their church. There will be songs and prayers asking God to take care of PJ's spirit. Prayers will also be said to help his family get through the 'missing'. Then they'll bring his body to the cemetery to be buried."

Before my dad could continue I asked my mom, "How come we didn't go to a memorial service or funeral for old Mr. Levine when he died? He was our friend, too."

Mom said that Mr. Levine was Jewish. Jews pray in a building called a Temple or Synagogue, not a Church or Meeting House. They, too, have different customs and ceremonies.

"There was a funeral for Mr. Levine. The Rabbi, the leader or teacher of the Jewish congregation, said prayers for him and his family. But there's an extra way that Jewish people honor their dead and deal with their sadness. It's a special time of seven days after the funeral and the burial. It's called 'Shiva', which means seven."

Dad continued, "We didn't go to the funeral for Mr. Levine, because we waited for Shiva. Mr. Levine's family stayed at his house for seven days, and friends visited them there."

Mom asked, "Do you remember when I baked the cake and we all went down to Mr. Levine's house to see his family? We told them what a good neighbor he'd been. Do you remember?" I nodded. "Well that visit was a 'Shiva call'. That was our special way of saying good-bye to Mr. Levine, and letting his family know we'd miss him, too."

"Now for the last part," my father continued, "before the Funeral Mass for PJ, there'll be something called a 'wake' or 'viewing' at a funeral home. It's just another way to visit the family of someone you cared about to let them know that you feel sad, too. The difference at a wake is that PJ's body will be there in a box called a casket or coffin. Sometimes it helps people to see the body for one last time and say good-bye that way."

"What will PJ look like dead?" I asked.

"He'll probably be in his best clothes and look like he's sleeping," my mom answered.

We all sat quietly for a while. Then Mom said, "It's very, very late. That's enough for tonight. Tomorrow we'll talk some more. You go and get ready for bed. Dad and I will be up to tuck you in."

For several weeks I'd been complaining that I was too big to be tucked in. That night I was so tired and sad, being tucked in felt pretty good. I stayed awake for a very long time, wondering about death and thinking about PJ.

CHAPTER 5

The next morning I didn't go downstairs right away. I started thinking again about all of the things that had happened the day before—PJ's accident, what *dead* meant, funerals, wakes, but most of all, the "missing." It was hard for me to get up and not think of things to do with PJ that day. What would it be like going back to school without him? We used to have a great time on the school bus. He wouldn't be there anymore.

I started to feel all upset again, so I got up, went to the bathroom, and washed my face. As I was brushing my teeth my mom called, "I have breakfast for you, as soon as you're ready."

When I got downstairs, I was surprised that I *could* eat. My insides felt like they were full of sadness. I didn't think there was any room for food.

Mom told me that Mrs. Gonzales had called. The wake and funeral for PJ were all planned. I wanted to hear what my mom was saying, but I still wished none of it was happening.

"You don't have to go to the wake or the funeral if you don't want to," Mom said. "You can say good-bye to PJ in your own special way." She continued, "If you *do* want to go, Dad and I will go with you. The wake is tonight, and the funeral is tomorrow morning."

Things were happening too fast! I was feeling angry that I had to decide about everything so soon. I was afraid that I would cry in front of other people, and I was a little afraid of seeing PJ dead, too. Just then, the phone rang. Mom answered it and said it was for me. The day *before* yesterday, I would have guessed it was PJ.

I picked up the phone and said, "Hello." It was Dan, a kid from my class. He and his best friend, Justin, used to play with PJ and me on the playground.

Dan said, "Justin and I were at the pool with my mom. We heard about PJ's accident. Everybody's talking about it. We just want you to know we're sorry you lost your friend."

"Thanks," I answered. It made me feel a little better to know that they felt sad, too. I told Dan what my parents had said about the "missing" hurting so much.

Dan said his mom called it "mourning." That's another word for the sadness and "missing" we all felt about PJ. Dan's mom had also told them about the wake and funeral. They'd heard that a lot of kids from school were going to the Church for the funeral.

Dan asked, "What are you going to do?"

I told him that I didn't know. "My mom and I are talking about it now. Can I tell you later?"

After I said good-bye to Dan, I told my mom what he'd said. The phone call had made me feel a little better. Dan and Justin cared about PJ—and me—too.

I asked, "Would it make the Gonzales family feel better if I go to the wake? It would let them know I cared about them."

Mom told me I didn't have to decide right away. She told me to take a little time. "What do you think PJ would want you to do?" she asked.

I went out the back door and into the yard. PJ and I had been saving up scrap wood to build a tree house. My dad had told us to pile it neatly and that he'd help us when we got enough. We had spent days drawing pictures of the tree house we wanted. I looked at the pile of wood, and started to cry again. It seemed wrong that it was a beautiful day, and that the sun was even shining!

I sat outside for a long time. I thought about PJ, and all the plans we'd made for that summer. None of those things would ever happen now because PJ was dead. I felt empty inside and almost mad at PJ for leaving.

I went inside the house and called my mom, "I think I'm angry at PJ for dying. I know he didn't do it on purpose. He didn't mean to die, but I'm mad at him for not being here."

Mom told me that it was OK to feel that way—for a while. She said that mourning or missing someone can make us feel sorry for *ourselves*. After all, we're the ones who've lost a friend.

"If I go to the wake tonight, what do I have to do?" I asked.

Mom told me that she had already called the director of the funeral home. She'd asked if PJ's young friends could come early. That way we could look around, have things explained to us, and then, if we wanted to, say any special prayers or good-byes at PJ's body in the coffin. The funeral director even said that I could bring something special to put in the coffin as a sign of my friendship with PJ.

I asked if PJ's family was going to be there. Would I be able to let them know I was sorry they were mourning?

"Yes," Mom said. "The wake is really for the family."

"Then I've decided to go to the wake with you and dad. PJ would want me to."

After lunch, my mom called Dan's mom to let the guys know I was going. When she got off the phone, Mom told me we were going to meet them at the funeral home at 6:30 that night.

I went upstairs to think about what I'd leave with PJ's body as a sign of our very special friendship.

CHAPTER 6

I looked around my room and was surprised to see how many things reminded me of PJ—the model rockets we'd made together, the posters I'd bought on our trips to the science center and the zoo, and the drawings of the tree house. When we were planning the tree house, PJ had found an old glass door knob. He insisted we put it on the drawings of the "only tree house in the world with a glass door knob." I opened my closet and looked for the box we'd put all the tree house stuff in. As I picked up the door knob I smiled, remembering how excited PJ was when he found it. I knew that *it* was what I would leave with PJ's body at the funeral home.

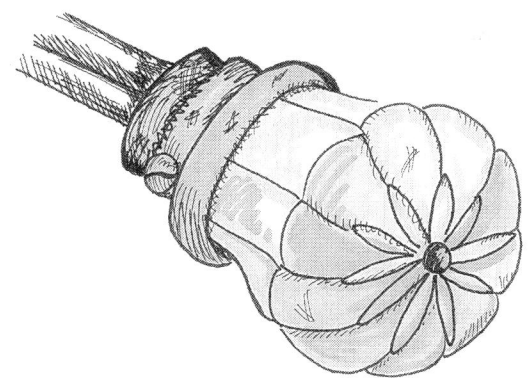

I got glass cleaner and made the door knob shine. Then I took the best drawing of our dream tree house down from my bedroom wall. At the bottom of the drawing I wrote, "PJ, thanks for being the best friend anyone could ever have." I wrapped the door knob in the drawing, sealed it with tape, and put it on my bed. I felt good knowing that I had something really special to leave at the funeral home that night.

My mom came in with my good shirt and pants. She told me that people get sort of dressed up to go to a wake. It was one way of showing respect for the family in mourning.

"What can I say to PJ's family tonight to make them feel better?" I asked.

"Not much honey," she answered. " The hurt they feel right now will take a long time to heal. The only thing anyone can say is 'I'm sorry'. As time passes, we can visit them and let them know we care about them."

I told Mom that I had my gift for PJ ready. I was glad that she didn't ask what it was. The door knob, wrapped in the drawing, was the last secret PJ and I could share. That was important to me.

The afternoon seemed very long that day. I thought about PJ a lot and wondered what the wake was going to be like. By the time my dad got home, I wasn't so sure I even wanted to go! As we ate dinner, Mom and Dad told me again that I didn't have to go if I didn't want to.

I was scared and sad about PJ, but I was also very curious about the whole thing. What would the funeral home be like, what would I say to PJ's family, but most of all, what would PJ look like dead? I told them I was going.

After dinner, Dad stayed in his suit from work and Mom and I went upstairs to change. I put on my good shirt and pants, picked up my good-bye gift for PJ, and went downstairs.

CHAPTER 7

The funeral home was big and beautiful with a fancy lawn and garden. We waited outside until Justin and Dan got there with Dan's mom. Nobody felt much like talking, so we went up the stairs together and into the funeral home.

The inside of the house was as pretty as the outside. The lights were dim, and it was cool and very quiet. A man came down the hall to welcome us and introduced himself. His name was Mr. Beck. He and his wife were directors of the funeral home. He told us he was glad we came early.

"Many grownups have questions about funeral homes and never get a chance to ask them," Mr. Beck said. "I like to meet with young people to explain things. It's hard enough to lose a friend like PJ without being confused by everything around you."

Mr. Beck told us that his job as a funeral director was to help PJ's family plan the wake, funeral, and burial of PJ's body. He helped arrange the Funeral Mass at PJ's church and the burial at the cemetery. If PJ's family had wanted his body burned, "cremation," Mr. Beck called it, he would have arranged for that, too.

"Different people honor their dead in different ways," he continued. "A funeral director's job is to see that things are done the way each family wants them."

Mr. Beck showed us that there were separate rooms for each family having a wake. In his funeral home, they could have four wakes at one time. The only wake that night was PJ's, so he took us to the largest room at the end of the hall.

At the door of the room there was a sign and a book on a stand. The sign said, "Paul Joseph Gonzales." It was really strange to see PJ's whole name written out. I knew that was his name, but even the teachers in school called him "PJ."

Mom told me the book was there so that everyone who visited the Gonzales family could sign their names. That way PJ's family would be able to remember all of the people who cared and came to see them. Our parents put their names in the book, but Dan, Justin and I signed for ourselves. I wanted PJ's family to know that I cared a whole lot.

As we finished signing our names, Miss Porter, our fourth grade teacher, came down the hall. She had three of the girls from my class with her. Jackie, Brittany and Sarah rode on my school bus. I was surprised to see them there because PJ and I used to tease them a lot. One time, when we were fooling around, Jackie hit PJ with her lunch box. He started bleeding, the bus driver got angry, and we all got into trouble.

They were at PJ's wake. I guess they knew we were only kidding.

Miss Porter looked very sad, and after she showed the girls how to sign the book, she walked over to me. "I am so sorry about PJ. I know that you two were very special friends. I'm sure you'll miss him a great deal."

I didn't know what to say, so my mom thanked Miss Porter for me.

Mr. Beck invited us into the room. Everyone was whispering, and the whole room smelled of the flowers that were everywhere. Mr. Beck explained that many people had sent the flowers to PJ's family.

"People want to let PJ's family know they care," he said. "Flowers are another way to express that caring or 'sympathy' to them."

There were couches around the sides of the room and chairs set up in the middle. Mr. Beck pointed out PJ's coffin at the front of the room. As he and the others started toward the front, I saw PJ's family sitting in chairs next to the coffin. I couldn't follow. I grabbed my dad's hand and just stood still. I was holding the wrapped door knob, trying hard not to cry, and wishing I was anywhere but there.

Dad stayed with me and my mom went up to see PJ's mom. Dad asked me if I wanted to go home. When I shook my head "No," he suggested that we sit in the back of the room for a while.

We sat on one of the big couches. I don't know what I was so afraid of. Maybe it was because I knew that seeing PJ's body in the coffin would mean he was really dead. I had to keep reminding myself, "it's only the package." PJ's spirit was free.

I watched the other kids go up to the coffin. Dad explained that the Catholics would kneel down to pray. The others would just stand there quietly for a few minutes. He whispered, "They're saying their prayers and good-byes to PJ."

I watched Mr. and Mrs. Gonzales get up from their chairs and speak to each adult and child. Miss Porter was crying quietly as she and the others followed Mr. Beck out of the room. The kids went into Mr. Beck's office to ask any questions they had before going home.

CHAPTER 8

My mom had been sitting with the Gonzales family. She came back to my dad and me, and asked if I was OK. She and Dad both said I didn't have to do anything more. We could go home.

"I'd like to talk to PJ's family, and I have my good-bye gift for PJ," I said. I guess I wanted to say my good-byes to PJ without all of the other kids around.

I took my mom's hand, and with my dad, we walked to the front of the room. Mrs. Gonzales cried as she hugged me. PJ's dad cried as he kissed me on both cheeks. PJ had told me once that in Cuba where his father was born, men always kissed each other on both cheeks. Maria said her little brother was lucky to have a friend like me. Even PJ's big brother, Don, hugged me. He told me he'd miss yelling at us for messing up his stuff.

Mrs. Gonzales walked to the coffin with me. I looked at PJ's body. Like my mom had said, he didn't look bad. He *did* have his best clothes on, and he *did* look asleep. Just in case, I watched his chest to see if he was breathing, but he didn't move at all. I knew that PJ was dead, but it wasn't as scary as I thought it would be.

I put the door knob in the corner of the coffin and said, "Bye, PJ. Thanks for being my friend."

Mrs. Gonzales put her arm around me. "He knew that you were his friend. That's the most important gift you can ever give anyone."

PJ was special and he was my friend. He was dead, but that wasn't what was so scary. I was missing him terribly and he wasn't coming back. *That* was the scary part.

Mr. Gonzales came over and said, "Always remember that you helped PJ to laugh and enjoy life. We thank you for that."

My parents joined us and we bowed our heads as Mr. Gonzales asked us to pray with him, "Dear God, please keep PJ's spirit safe in Your care and help all of us to get through this time of grieving."

I cried a little as we said good night to the Gonzales family, and walked down the hall. My mom gave me a tissue, and I had just finished wiping my eyes when two kids from my soccer team came in.

Marty and John were good guys, but I didn't want them to see me crying. PJ and I had played on the same team with them and *nobody* cried when they got hurt. I didn't want them to think I was a wimp.

They walked up to me and Marty said, "Gee, I'm really sorry about PJ. You must feel rotten. You guys were best friends."

I knew I couldn't talk about PJ, not then. I was glad when John added, "You two were great on the team. We wouldn't have won without you."

I *could* talk about soccer. "We had fun playing with you guys," I said. "Winning the trophy in our league and the team pizza party were a great way to end the season."

"Yeah," said Marty, "it'll be hard without PJ next year."

"Yeah," I said, "it'll be hard without PJ." My dad put his hand on my shoulder and I added, "I've got to go now. See you around." I turned, took a deep breath, and went down the steps with my parents.

I was surprised to see that it was still light outside. It seemed like we had been in the funeral home for a very long time. As we got to our car, I turned back and saw a lot of grown ups going in to see the Gonzales family. It seemed all wrong. PJ was dead, everyone inside was so sad, but the sun was still shining.

I didn't feel like talking. No one in the car did. When we got home, I sat in the living room with my parents. While my mom got us cold drinks, my dad told me that he wouldn't be able to go to PJ's funeral. Dad's an accountant at a bank and there was an important meeting in the morning that he couldn't miss. He told me that he'd be thinking of Mom and me, and remembering PJ, even at his desk.

Mom asked me if I still wanted to go to the funeral. She knew the wake had been very sad for me. "You don't have to go to the funeral, if you don't want to."

"Yes, I want to go. I have to finish it all up," I answered. All I'd thought about since PJ's accident was missing him and what it meant to be "dead." I guess I thought I'd feel better when the funeral was over. Boy, was I wrong!

After I got into bed that night, I felt so strange. It was still like a dream, a bad dream. So much had happened in only two days. My best friend had died. I'd learned about different ceremonies honoring the dead. I'd gone to a wake, and I was going to a funeral.

I was sure I'd be awake for a long time, but I wasn't. I fell asleep wondering how long the awful feeling of missing PJ would last.

CHAPTER 9

In the morning, I woke up as my dad came into my room. He gave me a hug, said it was very early, and promised to call me at lunch time.

I must have gone back to sleep, because the next thing I heard was Mom saying, "It's time to get up, Sleepyhead."

I washed up, put on my clothes, and went down to the kitchen. As I was finishing my cereal and orange juice, I spilled juice all over my shirt. For some goofy reason, I started to cry.

Mom smiled and said, "Well, I've heard the expression, 'Don't cry over spilled milk', but I never heard anything about spilled orange juice." That sort of made me smile.

"Don't worry about it," Mom said. "We have plenty of time. Your blue shirt is hanging in your closet. Go change and I'll clean up. When you come down, we can leave." I went upstairs, still surprised that I had cried because I'd spilled my juice.

I'd been to PJ's church once before. We'd had a Boy Scout ceremony there and PJ had showed me around. He went to Mass and Sunday School every week, while I went to Meeting for Worship and First Day School. Mom and

Dad said I could go with him one Sunday, but we'd never done it. Now it was too late.

As Mom and I got out of the car, I remembered what PJ had told me. Catholics name their churches after holy people called saints, who lived a long time ago. PJ's church was named after a man called "Saint Francis." Francis had been very rich, but he gave away all of his money to help the poor. He loved people and animals, too.

PJ liked the big statue of Saint Francis in front of the church, because it showed him with a bird in his hand and a baby deer at his feet.

Saint Francis Church was big and very different from our Friends Meeting House. As Friends, or Quakers, we have no statues or stained glass windows or even candles. PJ had come to Meeting for Worship with me once and I'd told him that Friends used to be called "plain" because our Meeting Houses are so simple.

PJ had been surprised that in our Meeting for Worship everyone sat in silence, with no music or leader. He told me that at Mass people prayed out loud, sang hymns, and the priest talked to everyone about God.

After Meeting that day, PJ and I went to First Day School. My teacher had told us that there are many ways to worship God. Both Quakers and Catholics believe that God lives in everyone. Catholics worship Him out loud with prayers and songs. Quakers sit silently in order to speak to God within themselves and within each other. Friends only speak out loud in Meeting for Worship when they feel led by God to share their thoughts or prayers.

Even though I'd been in Saint Francis Church before, I'd never been to Mass. As Mom and I walked in, there was music playing. As we got further into the church, I turned around and looked up. There was sort of a second floor like a balcony, and there were very large pipes going all the way to the ceiling. PJ had told me that the "second floor" was called a choir loft. It was where the woman who played the organ and the singers, or choir, stayed during the Mass.

He'd also said, "The large pipes are part of the organ and help to make it sound really cool."

When Mom and I sat down, I looked around and saw that the church was almost full. There were a lot of people I knew—kids from school, many of the teachers, and even Mr. Seymour, the principal, was there. PJ's family wasn't there though, and I asked my mom about it. She said that they would be coming in with the priest as he led PJ's coffin to the front of the church. I didn't understand but Mom said the priest would welcome PJ's body into Saint Francis for the last time. The words, "the last time" sounded awful!

Two older boys from our school, dressed in white robes, came out of a side door at the front of the church. They went around the front of the Church and lit some candles. PJ had told me that candles were lit right before Mass began. The boys went back inside and came out again with a man dressed in beautiful white robes. Mom told me that the robed man was the priest.

I thought black was the color for death—it always is in the movies. PJ's family had black clothes on at the wake, too. "How come the priest has white on?" I whispered.

Mom explained that black usually *is* the color of mourning. Even though we were all missing PJ, the priest wore white to celebrate PJ's life and the fact that his spirit is not dead. It was a way of reminding us that we should remember PJ with joy and happiness. I sort of understood, but at that moment I certainly didn't feel much joy or happiness.

As the priest walked to the back of the Church, Mom told me it was time to be quiet. The funeral was about to begin. She told me she'd answer my questions later.

I could hear the priest saying something at the back door of the Church but I couldn't hear the words. He started back in and then I saw PJ's family. Mr. and Mrs. Gonzales, Don and Maria, and PJ's grandparents were behind the priest. They looked terrible. They were crying and walking very slowly.

Behind them were Mr. Beck from the funeral home and, what I found out later, PJ's coffin. The coffin had been put on a stand with wheels, and the priest had covered it with a white cloth with a cross on top.

The rest of the ceremony, PJ's Funeral Mass, is all mixed up in my mind. The priest said a lot of prayers, there was the smell of what my mom called "incense," and there was singing. The priest stood up and talked to everyone. He talked to PJ's family first, and was very kind.

Then he talked to all the kids. He told us to remember PJ's smile and laughter and all of the wonderful times we'd had. He told us to remember that PJ was a good boy, that God loved him very much, and that we should be glad we'd had him for a friend.

The priest said that people often ask, "If God loves us, why would He let a child die?" I sat up and listened hard for the answer.

"I am absolutely sure that God loves each and every one of us, but I don't know the answer to that question," he continued. "People much wiser than I am have been searching for *that* answer for a long, long time. All I know is that God cares for us, and that He will help us get through the pain of losing PJ."

The priest ended by saying that he would pray for PJ's family and all of his friends. Then he went back and finished the funeral.

I had been waiting for someone to tell me *why* PJ had to die. When the priest finished talking, I realized that all of the grownups didn't know either.

The awful empty feeling came back again, and I knew that PJ's funeral wasn't going to "finish it all up." It was going to take me a long, long time to be able to think of him and not be sad.

I don't remember anything else about the funeral, except that when it was over a lot of people were crying. As my mom and I left the church she asked me if I wanted to go to the cemetery for the burial of PJ's body.

"No," I said. " Can we please go home?"

When we got home, Mom was fixing lunch when my dad called. I answered the phone, and he asked how the funeral went and if I was OK. I told him that the funeral made me even sadder and that I didn't want to go to the cemetery.

Dad told me, "It's all right that you didn't go to the cemetery. If you ever *do* want to go to see PJ's grave, I'll take you. You have lost your best friend, and this has been very hard for you. You've been great. Just know that your mom and I are very proud of you and love you very much."

I started crying again and gave my mom the phone. While she talked to my dad, I sat down to eat my lunch.

I picked up the peanut butter and strawberry jam sandwich my mom had made. As I took a bite, it made me remember the phone call about PJ's accident. I tried to eat some more, but the taste reminded me of PJ's death. Mom was off the phone by then and I saw her watching me as I put the sandwich down.

"I don't think I like strawberry jam anymore," I told her.

She asked if I wanted something else to eat. I said I wasn't very hungry and asked if I could go outside. She nodded and I went out into the backyard.

I felt as if my brain was tired. I didn't want to think about wakes, funerals, death, or even PJ for a while. I got my bike and helmet, yelled to my mom that I was going to the park, and took off down the driveway. The park is only a few blocks away and I like to ride there.

There's a bike path in the park where you can ride hard and fast. There's also a small pond hidden by trees, with a dock and lots of fish, tadpoles, and full grown frogs. When I got to the park, I rode around the bike path twice as fast as I could. It made me sweaty and out of breath. I went through the trees to the pond, and was glad to see that no one else was there. It's one of my best "private" places, even in the winter when it's all frozen over. That afternoon I got down on my belly on the dock, and just watched the insects, fish and others creatures that lived there.

I stayed that way for a long time and fell asleep. I woke up when I heard talking through the trees. It was a group of grownups I'd seen before. They meet every night to jog in the park. I got up, put on my helmet, and rode home.

CHAPTER 10

The next two weeks were horrible. I missed having PJ to play with and was either crying or angry most of the time. Mom and Dad tried to talk to me, but I didn't want to listen. I wanted to be left alone, but at the same time, I wanted them to pay attention to me and make the hurt go away.

My dad told me that it was OK to miss PJ and even to be angry. He told me that he and Mom loved me and were very sorry I was hurting. Dad said that only time would help my hurt to heal.

I was so cranky that my parents finally lost their patience. They told me that PJ's death gave me no right to be nasty, to them or anyone else, and I'd better shape up.

Part of my problem was that Mom was going back to work in August. I was supposed to go to day camp, but without PJ, I didn't want to go. Mom tried to get me excited about going—she even took me there one afternoon for a bike race.

All I said was, "Please, can we go home?" I didn't want to meet a new bunch of kids or even see kids I knew from school. I guess I was pretty hard on my parents that summer. They didn't know what to do with me, and neither did I.

Three days before Mom was due back at work, my grandmother called.

When I answered the phone, Grandma Peg said, "Hi, there. How's my favorite grandson?" She always calls me that because I'm her *only* grandson.

"I need a favor. I slipped on the back steps yesterday and sprained my ankle. Do you think you could help me out for a few weeks?"

Grandma Peg is really great. She still lives out in the country on the small farm where my dad grew up. She has chickens, two dogs, a goat named "Whiskers," and lots of cats in the barn.

"Grandma, are you OK? Can you walk?"

She laughed and said, "Well, I can walk, but I hobble. I look like I'm 102 years old! The doctor says my ankle will heal faster if I don't walk on it so much. If you can help with the chickens, take the dogs for their runs in the field, and try to keep Whiskers out of trouble, I think I can handle the rest."

"Oh, Grandma, I'll be able to help a whole lot. You'll be surprised at how much I can do. Wait, let me get Mom."

My mom got on the phone and I heard her asking Grandma Peg if she was all right. They talked for a while and Mom said she and Dad would talk it over, make plans, and call Grandma back that night.

When Mom hung up, she turned and said, "I'm so glad you offered to help your grandmother. Dad or I could take time off from work if we had to, but you're big enough now to really give her a hand. We'll call every couple of days to make sure you two are OK, but I think you and Grandma Peg will do just fine."

That night, when my dad came home from work, I was all excited, "I'm going to go help Grandma Peg on the farm."

"Whoa, slow down. What's going on?" he asked.

Mom told him about his mother's injured ankle and her request for help. We talked about what I'd need to pack and when we'd be able to leave. It's a good thing it was a Friday night. It meant we had the weekend to drive to the farm.

My dad called Grandma Peg and told her he was sorry about her ankle. He also told her that we had started packing and would leave by noon the next day.

It takes four hours to get to the farm. Mom and Dad would drive me there, stay overnight on Saturday, and then drive back home on Sunday. That way, my dad wouldn't miss any days at work, and Mom would be back in time to return to her job on Monday.

Things were crazy around our house that night as we planned, packed and rushed around. I didn't realize it then, but it was the first time since PJ's death that I was excited and looking forward to something.

We all got to bed very late. Mom had packed food and dad helped me pack my stuff for the farm. He laughed and told me how *he* used to help during the summer when he was growing up.

"It was different when my father was alive," he told me. "The farm was bigger then. Your Grandpa and

Grandma worked hard and we had to hire other people to help. When Grandpa died, Grandma Peg knew she couldn't manage it all by herself. She sold some of the land and has kept the small farm going all these years."

"How old were you when your father died?" I asked.

"I was eighteen and just starting college. Grandma Peg called me and told me that he'd had a heart attack and was in the hospital. I got home in time to see him and talk to him one more time. Grandpa died of another heart attack the day after I got home."

Dad had never told me about his father's death before. I guess I wouldn't have understood. That night, because of PJ's death, I knew what it felt like to lose someone you cared about.

"I'm glad you had a chance to talk to Grandpa before he died," I said, as I packed up my fishing pole.

My dad stopped packing, and looked at me for a long time. "Thanks, son," was all he said.

The ride to Grandma Peg's didn't seem as long as I remembered. Maybe it's because I slept most of the way. I was very tired from being up so late the night before.

"We're almost there," my mom called from the front seat. "Wake up and have a cold drink with us."

I stretched, rubbed my eyes and looked around. We were in farm country all right. "How much longer?" I asked.

Dad answered, "About twenty more minutes."

Mom gave me some pretzels and lemonade, and I watched as we passed the farmers' fields. The corn was tall and green and the wheat was waving in the wind.

I felt almost good for the first time since PJ's accident. Some of the hurt inside me seemed to be melting. I thought how strange it was to feel good again. I didn't have long to think though. As we pulled into Grandma Peg's, the dogs, the goat, and even the chickens came to greet us.

When we got near the house, my grandmother came out on the back porch. She had a pair of crutches and she was right. She hobbled.

"Welcome. Welcome. Welcome," she called. "It's great to see my favorite grandson arrive." Dad stopped the car and I jumped out and ran to give my Grandma Peg a big hug.

"Careful, now. You're so big, you just might knock an old lady over," she said.

I laughed, "Oh Grandma, you're not an old lady. You told me you'll *never* be an old lady, because 'age is only a number'. Remember when you said that?"

"Good grief, child. Do you remember everything I say?" Then she hugged me so tight it took my breath away.

My parents joined us on the porch. There was lots of hugging and they asked my grandmother about her ankle. She said it was much better, now that we'd arrived.

That weekend flew by. Before we knew it, it was time for Mom and Dad to drive home. As they drove out of the farm waving good-bye to Grandma Peg and me, I felt a little sad. I'd never really been away from my parents before. I was excited about staying with my grandmother, but it was strange watching them leave.

I guess my grandma knew. She put her arm around my shoulder and said, "Come on in, now. We'll have something to eat and plan our chores for tomorrow."

CHAPTER 11

I'll never forget that August. I worked harder than I ever thought I could and had a great time doing it! Grandma Peg kept me busy every minute of the day and I was so tired at night I usually fell right to sleep.

We talked a lot that summer, my grandmother and me. I remember one day while we were cleaning the chicken coop I asked her, "Do you ever worry about dying?"

She looked at me and answered, "I used to, right after your grandfather died. It took me a while to realize that 'worrying about dying' was messing up my *living*. I will always love and miss your grandpa, but I'm still alive. There are other people who need my love, and who love me. I can't cheat them, or myself, so I made up my mind to get busy *living*."

I didn't say anything, because on the nights I didn't go right to sleep, I'd been worrying a whole lot about dying. Grandma was right, it was certainly messing up *my* living.

Another talk we had was after I'd chased Whiskers most of the day. Goats can get into so much trouble! That day, he'd eaten part of the neighbor's wash. It was my fault, too—I'd left the gate open. Whiskers saw the wash hanging on the line to dry and decided to take a walk and have a "snack."

By the time I caught him I was hot and sweaty and angry. I guess I was more angry at myself for leaving the gate open than I was at the dumb old goat. I was crying as I brought him home and put him in the barn.

"Now, just look at you," my grandma said. "You let an old goat 'get *your* goat'. The things he ate can be replaced, and you got him back safe and sound. Why are you so angry?"

"Because I left the gate open. How can I be so stupid?" I growled.

"You paid for your mistake by chasing and catching Whiskers," she said. "Welcome to the human race," she continued. "Human beings make mistakes. That's why we put erasers on pencils."

I was still pouting when she added, "There's no shame in making a mistake. The shame is when we don't learn from our mistakes. I'll bet you never forget to close the gate again."

My grandma was right. For the rest of the summer, I always checked to see that I had closed the gate behind me—sometimes I even checked twice! Whiskers was able to get into mischief all by himself. He never got any help from me again.

My favorite job on the farm was taking the two dogs, Salt and Pepper, for long runs in the fields. There was a stream in the woods that was as good for thinking as the pond in the park back home. On hot days, the dogs loved to splash in the pond, and we'd all get soaking wet. Then I'd flop down at the side of the stream, watch the water flow by, and listen to the bubbling noises it made. Sometimes Salt and Pepper settled down, too.

It was there one day, with both dogs lying beside me, that I realized I hadn't thought about PJ for a while. The awful feeling inside me was disappearing, just as my mom had said it would. That night I asked my grandmother, "Is it wrong to stop hurting when someone dies? Does it mean you don't care about them anymore?"

"Are you talking about your friend, PJ?" she asked. Grandma had never talked to me about PJ before. I guess she knew about his accident but I was glad that up until then she had never mentioned it.

"Yeah," I replied. "Today, in the woods, I thought about him for the first time in days. I feel a little guilty for forgetting him."

"I don't really think you *forgot* him," she answered." You'll never *forget* PJ. As you grow, and new things happen in your life, you won't think of him as often as you did. It won't hurt so much when you do either. But that doesn't mean you've stopped missing him or caring about *his* dying. It just means that you've decided to get on with *your* living."

Like I said, Grandma Peg is really great!

CHAPTER 12

The month went by so fast. Grandma Peg's ankle was almost all better and we were able to take long walks in the woods. Sometimes we talked, and sometimes we didn't. It was just good to be together in the sunshine, or even in the rain.

Mom and Dad had called every few days as they had promised. But when they called and said it was almost time for school to start, I wasn't ready. I'd always liked school, but the thought of going back without PJ made my insides hurt again.

"Having to do things alone that you used to do with PJ will make the hurt come back, but only for a little while," Grandma said. "Just remember all of our talks. Remember to keep busy *living*."

It's funny—I was sad when my parents left me at the farm, and I was sad when they came to pick me up. Oh, I was really glad to see *them*, but I'd had a wonderful time and I would miss my Grandma Peg.

Mom and Dad said I had "grown a foot" and looked wonderful. My grandmother told them I had been a big help and thanked them for "loaning me to her." I laughed at being "loaned" and told my parents what a great time I'd had.

"Maybe next year I can come for the whole summer, Grandma. You won't have to hurt your ankle or anything. I'll just come to help."

Grandma hugged me hard, "You're welcome here any time you want to come. Remember though, I'm coming to your house for Thanksgiving."

We had a fun ride home. I talked and talked about Salt and Pepper, Whiskers, the chores on the farm, and Grandma Peg. Dad laughed at my stories, and then he told some funny stories of his own. The goat they had when he was a kid, "GP," for garbage pail, got into as much trouble as Whiskers. My mom just laughed at both of us.

As we got close to home, it felt good to be "almost there." I'd had a great time on the farm, but when we pulled in our driveway, the house looked great.

Dad said, "As soon as we've unpacked the car, we have a surprise for you."

I was really curious, so I rushed to get everything into the house. Mom said she'd order a pizza for supper while Dad showed me the surprise. He told me to close my eyes and take his hand. I was laughing as I did what he asked.

My dad turned me in a few circles, then led me outside. We walked a little way, then he said, "You can open your eyes now."

There, in my own backyard, was the best basketball hoop I'd ever seen. There were even markings on the ground, like on a gym floor.

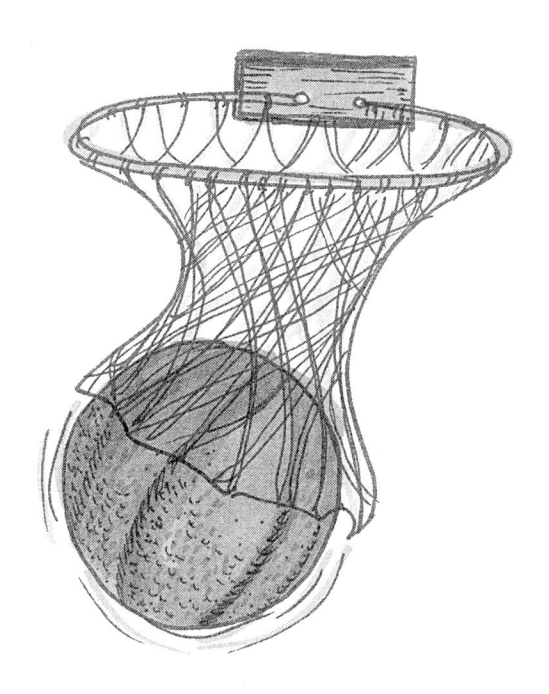

"We had talked about getting you a basketball hoop, so I worked on it the whole time you were away," Dad said. "I hope you like it."

"Like it? It's fantastic!" I shouted. "Thank you, thank you, thank you!"

Mom came out into the yard with a brand new basketball in her hands. She threw it to me and said, "OK, let's see what you can do with this."

We had our pizza outside and spent the rest of the evening shooting, or at least trying to shoot, baskets.

The next morning, we went to Meeting for Worship. I was surprised at First Day School when so many kids told me they'd missed me. They were glad to see that I was back. I told them all about the farm and my stories made them laugh.

When we got home and were having lunch, Mom said, "We have three days to get you ready for school."

Since Mom was back at work, I was staying next door with Mrs. Olson during the day. I always stayed there when school was closed if my parents were at work. The Olsons had three year old twins and Mrs. Olson treated me like a big kid. I had fun helping her, and was close enough to run home if I wanted to.

Mom continued, "Tomorrow, when I get home from work, we can go shopping for school supplies."

"OK, I'll be ready. I'll have the twins watching for you," I told her.

The next morning, the twins, Ellen and Elizabeth, got all excited when I arrived at their house. Mrs. Olson told me they had missed me while I was away and asked if I'd had a good time at my grandmother's. I told her it had been great, but it was good to be home.

The twins loved it when I played in the sandbox with them, so Mrs. Olson and I took them outside. I made castles for Ellen and then helped Elizabeth knock them down. They were twins, but they were very different. Ellen was always clean and neat, and Elizabeth managed to get dirty before she even got out of the house.

At lunchtime, Mrs. Olson made a sandwich for me but I couldn't eat it. It was peanut butter and strawberry jam. She didn't know about the strawberry jam.

"I think I'd rather have just plain peanut butter," I told her. "I don't like strawberry jam anymore."

Mrs. Olson said, "No problem. I'll eat that one and make you another sandwich."

I like Mrs. Olson, but I was glad I didn't have to explain about the strawberry jam. Maybe I would, someday.

While the twins took a nap, I went over to my yard to shoot baskets. I played for a while, and stopped when I heard laughing. Ellen and Elizabeth were up. They were watching me run around the basketball hoop and laughing their heads off.

I went back to the Olson's, had a glass of iced tea, and I told the twins to watch for my mom. She gets home from work at about 4 o'clock.

It was funny when my mom pulled into our driveway. Elizabeth and Ellen started waving the minute they saw her. I told the twins I'd be back tomorrow and went over to meet my mom.

The mall was really crowded. Everyone was getting ready for the opening of school. I got new sneakers, two really cool notebooks and a great backpack. Mom bought me an ice cream cone, but she wasn't feeling very well and didn't want one. Her stomach had been upset all day, and she thought it was from the pizza we'd had the night before.

"Gee, Mom, I feel fine," I said. "Sorry you don't feel so good."

When we got home, Mom told my dad and me that she was going to rest for a little while. We told her we'd eat leftovers for dinner, and to let us know if she needed anything.

While we were eating, I showed Dad what we'd bought that afternoon. He asked me if I was excited about starting school.

"Yeah, I guess so. But I'm a little worried about going back to school without PJ."

"I can understand that." said Dad. "It will probably be hard for a little while because your whole school routine will be different. I think you'll discover though, that you have more friends at school than you realize."

"I hope you're right," I said.

I went to Olson's the next day, even though Mom was home. She still didn't feel very good, and I decided to let her have peace and quiet. Besides, Ellen and Elizabeth were waiting for me.

It rained all day, so Mrs. Olson let us have popcorn and watch cartoons. I acted like I was watching the cartoons for the girls, but I really thought some of them were pretty funny.

CHAPTER 13

Wednesday morning, the first day of school, finally arrived. Both Mom and Dad stayed home long enough to see the school bus arrive. As I got on, I waved at them and turned to face a lot of the kids I hadn't seen since PJ's funeral. Most of them said "Hi" or waved, and I went and sat down. I purposely didn't go to the back of the bus because that's where PJ and I used to sit together.

Mrs. Harrison, our new teacher, met us on the playground. All the kids in our school like Mrs. Harrison. She walked us into the classroom, welcomed us back to school, and then introduced the new kids.

There were three new kids in our class that year—Matt, a boy who'd moved from New Jersey, and two new girls, Betsy and Raisa. Betsy was from Florida and Raisa had moved all the way from India.

When Mrs. Harrison asked them if they had anything they wanted to tell us, Matt and Betsy told us about their families, why they'd moved, and their old schools.

Raisa just looked very shy and said, "No, thank you," when Mrs. Harrison asked her if she had anything to say.

The rest of the day was spent getting our new books, the cafeteria schedule and menu for September, and a lot of notices to take home to our parents.

Nobody mentioned PJ. I was relieved, but sort of sad. The new school year had started without him and nobody seemed to notice.

That night I showed Mom and Dad my new books, gave them all the notices, and told them about the new kids in my class. Mom looked at everything, but still wasn't feeling real good, so she went to bed early. My dad and I played a video game until it was time for me to go to bed. He even let me win once in a while.

I have to admit that school was fun, and I was learning a lot. In gym, we were learning how to play full court basketball. Matt, the new kid, was really good. I told him about the hoop in my backyard and he asked if he could come over and play sometime.

Mrs. Harrison made us work hard, but if we were good all week, she read us great stories on Friday afternoon. If we misbehaved during the week, she made us make up the work instead of reading to us.

Whenever she said, "Class, if you can't settle down, we'll have to do this work on Friday afternoon," we knew what she meant. We usually got back to work in a hurry.

Before long it was October and we were planning a Halloween party at school. I told Mom about it, but didn't have any ideas for a costume. I wanted a great costume, but I didn't want to draw too much attention to myself.

Since school had started, I sort of stayed by myself. Dan and Justin had tried to be friends on the playground but it wasn't the same without PJ. I hadn't even invited Matt over to play basketball.

A few times some of the kids made fun of me. They thought I was being a snob and said things that hurt. "Oh, you think you're too good to play with the rest of us?" I didn't even get mad. I just got sad. How could they understand how different it was for me without PJ?

The week before Halloween, I decided to try and join the class fun. Maybe it would be easier in a costume. I decided that I wanted to be a robot. Dad brought some empty boxes home from the bank, we used old dryer hose for my arms, and I had my old soccer pads on my knees and dad's old boots. We sprayed everything with silver paint. Mom made antennae and we even sprayed her garden tools for my hands. We glued buttons and other stuff on a panel for my chest so it looked like dials and gadgets. By the time we finished, my robot costume looked really good.

The Halloween party at school was lots of fun—I even won a prize. That night, I went "trick or treating" in my costume, but only around my own neighborhood. I did get lots of candy and other goodies.

When we got home, Mom was resting again. I don't think I'd paid attention to it until that night, but Mom had been "resting" a lot. When I went up to bed, I started to worry that maybe Mom was really sick. I got all scared again, about death, and lay awake for a long time.

Mom seemed OK in the morning, so I sort of forgot about it.

I'd visited PJ's family a couple of times. Mr. and Mrs. Gonzales were glad to see me, and asked all kinds of questions about school. It was hard for me to tell them any of the fun stuff though; I was afraid they'd feel bad because PJ wasn't there.

CHAPTER 14

In the beginning of November, Mrs. Harrison asked me if I could stay after school one day. She'd call my mom to let her know I'd be late, and make sure I got on the last school bus. I said OK, but wondered why I had to stay. After the other kids left, I asked her if I'd done something wrong.

"Oh, no," she answered. "It's just that I've been a little worried about you. Your school work is fine, but you don't seem to want to work or play with your classmates very much."

"I like the other kids Mrs. Harrison, but sometimes I'd just rather do things by myself," I explained.

"Working alone is fine, but you almost seem to avoid the others. Could wanting to be by yourself have anything to do with your friend, PJ?" Mrs. Harrison asked. "I know that you two were best friends, and that he died last summer. PJ's death must have been very sad for you."

"Yeah," I said, sort of angry that she was talking about PJ. "What does PJ have to do with *now*, and the other kids? He isn't here."

"In a way, PJ *is* here. He's here in your mind and heart, because you'll always remember how special he was. But you also remember how much it hurt to lose him. None of us like to get hurt," Mrs. Harrison continued. "Sometimes, when we lose one friend, we won't make any others. That way, we don't have to be afraid of losing someone again."

I thought about what my teacher was saying and answered, "I don't know. I still miss PJ and all of the good times we had, but I don't know if I'm afraid."

"That's all right," Mrs. Harrison said. "Losing a good friend is very sad, it takes time to heal. I was wondering though, if you'd be willing to help one of your classmates?"

"Me, help someone else? Who do you want me to help?" I asked.

"Raisa. She is very shy, and hasn't made any friends here yet. She could use some help in math and I thought you two could make flash cards and go over them together."

"Oh," I said, "that would be easy. But Raisa is sort of different, and she's always alone. What will she think?"

Mrs. Harrison had already asked Raisa about working with me. Raisa had said that she would.

"Well, if Raisa says it's OK, I guess it's all right," I nodded.

We walked to the school bus and Mrs. Harrison thanked me and said good-bye. All the way home, I thought over her questions about PJ and about helping Raisa. I decided to wait until Thanksgiving to talk to Grandma Peg about being afraid of new friends. I wondered how Raisa felt being so alone.

The next day, Raisa and I started working together. She was very smart, but the math problems got her confused. We had fun making the flash cards—she even smiled once or twice. As the weeks passed by, she told me about her family.

Raisa's father worked with computers. They had moved to London, England, and then to the United States because of his job. She lived with her parents, her big brother, Raj, who was in high school, and her grandparents.

She was quiet most of the time and didn't say very much. When Raisa *did* talk, I found out that I liked talking with her. She told me lots of things about India and England.

One day, when we were drawing pictures of turkeys and Pilgrims, Raisa told me that people outside of the United States don't celebrate Thanksgiving. "It's an American holiday," she said.

I didn't know that before, but it made sense. The Pilgrims came to America and it was here that they celebrated the harvest with the Native Peoples who lived in this country before them.

I had fun telling Raisa all about Thanksgiving, about the turkey dinner, the parades on TV and having lots of company. I told her how Americans, no matter where they come from, or how they worship God, give thanks for all the good things we have in our country.

I also told Raisa about Grandma Peg and that she was coming for the holiday. Raisa was very close to her grandparents so she understood how much my grandmother meant to me.

The day before Thanksgiving, Mom gave me a basket of fruit for Raisa and her family. Mom had put a card on the basket. The card said in big letters "Happy First Thanksgiving." Raisa smiled when she read it, and told me that her family would be very pleased.

As we were leaving school that day, Raisa wished me "Happy Thanksgiving. I hope you have a nice visit with your grandmother."

CHAPTER 15

When I got home, I saw Grandma Peg's car in the driveway. I ran in the house yelling, "Where's my favorite grandmother?"

Mom and Grandma Peg came out of the kitchen. Mom said, laughing, "You'd better not let your other grandmother hear you say that."

My other grandmother lives in Florida and I call her "Nana." I said, "I'll just tell her that she's my favorite *Nana*." They laughed at that.

Grandma Peg gave me a big hug and we all went back into the kitchen. The kitchen smelled of pumpkin pie, there was a big turkey in the sink, and my grandmother was peeling a big pile of potatoes. I love Thanksgiving!

"Who's coming for dinner tomorrow?" I asked. Dad had to set up a large table in the living room, because we usually had at least ten people come for dinner. Grandma Peg was the only relative who lived close enough to come, so my parents always invited Quakers from Meeting, or people they knew at work who had no family nearby. Our Thanksgiving dinners were always great.

"Well," Mom said, " help me to count: Miss Sherman from Dad's office at the bank, Mr. Stillman from my office, with his wife and son, and the Pearsons from Meeting. How many does that make?"

The Pearsons have three children; they were in First Day School with me. I added up everyone and said, "Wow, that's thirteen people—seven grown ups and five kids. It will be a full house. I hope Dad has a big enough table."

Mom told me that she had called PJ's family to invite them to come, too. Mrs. Gonzales thanked her for the invitation but said they'd decided to go out to eat. They'd already made reservations at a restaurant.

The rest of the day was spent getting ready for the holiday. I helped Dad set up the table and then we put on the tablecloth and all the dishes, silverware and glasses. Mom had made a basket of fruit for us, too. When she put it in the middle of the table, Grandma Peg said, "Now, that's a real Thanksgiving table!"

The next morning I slept late. I woke up to the smell of turkey cooking and the sounds of talking and laughing in the kitchen. When I went downstairs, we all had "brunch," a combination of breakfast and lunch. We weren't having dinner until 5 PM, so I ate a lot. I didn't want to starve while I smelled the turkey!

The whole day was good. Dinner was delicious, all our guests were fun, and the Pearsons had rented a movie. After we ate, the adults sat around and talked and the kids watched the movie. Everyone helped to clean up, so there wasn't much to do when all the company left.

We were sitting in the living room, tired and stuffed, after Dad and I put the big table away. Mom told Grandma Peg and me that she had a surprise for us.

"We have many things to be thankful for today but there's something else," Mom said. "We're going to have a baby, early in May. Next year at Thanksgiving there'll be a new member of this family sitting at the table with us."

My grandmother got up and hugged my mom—she even cried a little bit.

I didn't know what to say. "You mean you're not sick?" I asked my mom.

"Oh, no, I'm not sick. I'm sorry if you were worried," she said. "Sometimes, when a woman is pregnant and the baby is growing inside her, she gets very, very tired. That's why I've been resting so much."

"Wow, a new baby in our house! I'm going to be a big brother!" I realized. "I can help, too. I've learned a lot helping Mrs. Olson with the twins next door."

It was a wonderful Thanksgiving. I never thought of PJ at all. As I was falling asleep I thought, "I'll have to talk to Grandma Peg about that."

CHAPTER 16

We had good talks that weekend, my grandma and me. The best was when I took her to the park and showed her my "secret" pond. I knew she'd like it, too.

I asked her about having good times and not missing PJ so much anymore. Was it wrong?

"That's what *getting busy living* is all about," she told me. "Life goes on and good things happen. PJ wouldn't want you to miss them."

I also told her about Mrs. Harrison and asked Grandma Peg if she thought I was "afraid" to make new friends.

"I don't think you're afraid. I just think you need some time. Besides, it sounds as if the girl you've been telling me about, Raisa, is a new friend."

"Oh, wait, Grandma," I told her. "Raisa's not a friend like PJ."

She looked at me and said, "Nobody will *ever* be a friend like PJ. He was 'one of a kind'." "But," she added, "we're all 'one of a kind'. If you give people a chance, you'll have new friends—not like PJ—but special, because they are 'one of a kind', too."

Grandma Peg always listened and I was sorry when she had to go back to the farm. She'd be with us at Christmas though, and she'd already told Mom that she'd come to help when the baby was born. I love my Grandma Peg—she's "one of a kind," for sure.

When I got back to school, I told Raisa about the baby. She was really excited and told me I was very lucky. I also asked Matt if he wanted to come over and shoot baskets sometime. He was glad that I invited him and we made plans for him to come. I still didn't feel right with Dan and Justin though. I guess it's because they reminded me of other times, with PJ.

After Thanksgiving, everyone in school started talking about our winter vacation. There were Christmas and Hanukkah decorations all over the place. I knew that the Jewish kids in school didn't celebrate Christmas, and that the Hanukkah decorations were for their holiday.

I didn't know about Raisa though, and I asked her what she wanted for Christmas. "I'm Hindu, and we don't celebrate Christmas," she told me. "One of our names for God is 'Shiva'. Hindus celebrate feasts in His life."

"Shiva" sounded like the word Mom used when we talked about mourning for Mr. Levine. I was confused and

81

asked Dad about it that night. He said that the words are spelled the same, but do sound different.

"The Jewish word, 'Shiva' sounds like 'give' with an 'a' on the end. It comes from Hebrew, the very old language of the Jews," he told me. "The Hindu name for God, 'Shiva', sounds like 'shee-va'. It comes from Hindi, another very old language."

"Boy," I said, "learning about other people is interesting, but sometimes it mixes up my brain."

My dad laughed, "Just think of all of the people you haven't met yet!"

Matt came over a couple of times before Christmas to play basketball. He taught me some new shots. I didn't want to play in the soccer league that year so I was glad to have a new game to play. Besides, I could shoot baskets all by myself.

Matt and I talked about playing together during vacation if it didn't snow. Basketball in the snow doesn't work.

"If it does snow," Matt asked one day, "is there a good place around here to go sledding?"

"Boy, is there ever!" I told him. "PJ and I used to go to the big hill on the golf course all the time. It's great!"

Matt stopped shooting baskets and asked, "Who's PJ?"

I'd forgotten that Matt had never known PJ. "He was my best friend since I was little," I said. "He died last summer, before you moved here."

"That must be tough," Matt replied, "to have your best friend die."

I just nodded.

Then Matt threw the basketball at me and said, "Try that long shot again." I was glad he didn't ask more about PJ and that he seemed to understand.

I'd been thinking about PJ a lot, because Christmas was coming. Every other year, PJ and I had written out our "wish lists" together. Christmas morning, we'd call each other to say, "What'd you get?"

Three days before Christmas, Mom and I went over to PJ's house. We brought Christmas cookies, and while we were there, we told the Gonzales family about the baby coming. They had a present for me—a neat pair of binoculars, and were happy to hear about the baby. It was a sad visit though; their house seemed so empty.

Mrs. Gonzales told us that she just couldn't put up a Christmas tree. PJ had been the youngest, and he always helped to pick out their tree. "It's just too soon," she said. "Maybe next year."

As I hugged them all good-bye and wished them Merry Christmas, I felt sorry for PJ's family. I wished real hard that by next Christmas the Gonzales house would be happy again.

CHAPTER 17

Grandma Peg came, we put up our tree, and I helped Dad to put the lights on the outside of the house. It looked wonderful!

Mom said, "This year, when we celebrate the birth of the Baby Jesus, we have our own new baby to look forward to."

On Christmas Eve, we went to the Meeting House to sing carols and celebrate with hot cider and donuts. All of the kids were really excited about Christmas, and while we were there it started to snow. As we left to go home, the Meeting House, with all of the old trees around it, looked like a Christmas card.

I was so excited I could hardly sleep. I knew that the sooner I fell asleep, the sooner I would wake up. Then I'd go downstairs and see what was under the tree.

I woke up and looked out my window. It had stopped snowing and everything was white and glistening in the early morning sunshine. I'd slept much later than I thought I would. Most Christmas mornings, I'd been up when it was still dark.

The house was quiet, so I tiptoed down the stairs. The tree was lit and there were lots of presents under it. They were all wrapped in colorful Christmas paper and everything looked magical. I heard a noise in the kitchen, and went in to find my grandma making coffee.

"Merry Christmas, favorite grandson," she said.

"Merry Christmas, favorite grandma," I answered.

We started laughing, gave each other a big hug, and went in to wake up my parents.

Mom, Dad and Grandma got coffee, I got hot chocolate, and we went to open the presents.

It was fantastic! I got a new bike helmet, a hockey stick, some games and books, and of course, clothes. Grandma Peg gave me new ice skates and there was lots of little stuff in my stocking.

I'd been saving my allowance for months, and when Grandma came at Thanksgiving, she'd helped me get presents for my parents. My dad likes to work with wood, so we got him a new set of drill bits. Mom's belly was getting big because of the baby, so we'd bought her a fluffy, new, BIG bathrobe. They were both surprised and happy when they opened their presents.

I'd had a problem with Grandma Peg's present. I wanted something very special for her, but as Christmas got closer and closer, I still didn't have any idea of what to get. One day in school, I'd told Raisa about it.

She said, "You had such a good time on your grandmother's farm. You even brought all of your photos in to show the class. Why don't you write a book for her, telling her how wonderful it was? You could draw some pictures and put in some of the photos."

It was a great idea! We told Mrs. Harrison about it and she helped, so it would be a surprise for my parents, too. I had barely finished the book in time and had it hidden in my room.

After all of the other presents had been opened I said, "Grandma Peg, I have to go upstairs to get *your* present," and I went to my room.

I had wrapped it myself and my grandma opened it slowly. When she saw what it was, she started to cry, "It's the most wonderful gift. You made it yourself. It's a book of memories. Thank you for putting so much love into it."

The phone rang and I got up to answer it. I felt strange because it was about the same time that PJ used to call on Christmas morning. "Hello," I answered.

"Merry Christmas, it's Matt. I just had to call and tell you that I got a new sled. When can we go to the big hill on the golf course?"

Matt said his dad could go sledding with us the next day. I told him to hold on and asked my dad about it. Dad said he'd be glad to go, too. We decided to meet at school the next morning.

CHAPTER 18

Christmas at our house is quiet. It's not like Thanksgiving when we have lots of company. After dinner, Mom and Dad went for a walk in the snow, and Grandma Peg and I made a snowman. We used parts of my Halloween costume and made him look like a "space snowman."

My parents got back from their walk and complimented us on our work. The snowman was terrific.

When we got him all finished, Grandma said, "Making snowmen is sort of like making friends, you know."

I didn't understand what she meant and asked, "What do you mean, Grandma?"

"Well, we like making snowmen *and* friends, and enjoy having them while they're with us. But snowmen melt, and sometimes, friends go away. We don't get to keep them forever."

"You mean PJ, don't you, Grandma?" I asked.

"Yes, but there are other times when friends go away. I'm sure Raisa and Matt had to leave friends behind when they came here. I'll bet their old friends miss them, too."

I thought about what she was saying. I'd never asked Matt or Raisa about the friends they had before they'd moved.

My grandmother went on, "If we worry about losing them, we'd never make snowmen *or* friends."

"But it's awful to lose a friend, Grandma."

"I know," she replied. "But it would be even more awful if we never had any."

I looked at Grandma Peg, "This is what Mrs. Harrison was trying to tell me, isn't it?"

My grandma started walking toward the house and turned back to say, "You're catching on. Now come on in for some hot chocolate."

The next day, Matt and I had a great time on our sleds. We met him and his dad at the school, put all the sleds in our car, and my dad drove to the golf course. Our dads even rode down the hill with us a few times. After sledding, we all stopped for pizza.

When we got back to their car, and Matt and his dad were putting their sleds in the trunk, I asked, "Matt, want to go to the movies during vacation?"

Matt looked at his dad, who nodded and said, "That's a great idea!"

Grandma Peg took us to the movies later that week. We ate popcorn and laughed through the whole movie. Matt thought my grandma was great and she liked him, too.

During that vacation, we also started working on the room for the baby. There was a room next to my parent's bedroom that Dad had been using as an office. Mom told me the baby would sleep in their room at first, then move into the old office.

Grandma Peg helped Mom clean up my old crib, dresser and high chair. Dad and I moved stuff out of the office and I helped when he painted the walls.

Dad said, "Since we don't know if the baby is a boy or a girl, yellow is a good color for the walls."

I asked him what that meant. He told me that some people use pink for girls and blue for boys. Yellow would be good either way.

I had gone to Mom's doctor with her a few times. The nurse let me put on the stethoscope and showed me how to put it on my mom's belly. I heard the baby's heart beating. Mom also let me put my hand on her stomach when the baby moved, so I could feel it kick. I was getting excited about having a baby brother or sister and was anxious to see what *it* was.

Grandma Peg laughed at me and said, "You'll just have to wait and see."

CHAPTER 19

The first day back at school, Raisa wasn't there. I didn't say anything, but the next day she wasn't there either. I waited until the others kids were gone, and on my way to the bus, I asked Mrs. Harrison if Raisa was OK.

"I'm sorry to have to tell you this, but Raisa's grandfather died. She won't be back until next week."

I got very upset. Mrs. Harrison asked me if I wanted to stay and talk. She'd call my mom and I could take the late bus home.

"No, I just want to go home," I told her, and ran for my bus.

I didn't talk to anyone on the bus. When I got home I ran inside, calling for my mom. She came from the kitchen, drying her hands on a towel.

"What's all the fuss about? You're yelling so loud I almost dropped our dinner."

I started crying, "Raisa's the one who gave me the idea for Grandma Peg's Christmas present. Her grandparents moved here with her, so she understood how much Grandma Peg means to me. Oh, Mom, I found out today that Raisa's grandfather died. I feel so sorry for her."

"I know you do," Mom said. "You probably know better than anyone how sad Raisa feels right now. I don't know much about Hindu funeral customs but I'll find out. I'm sure Raisa will be glad to have you as a friend, and we'll let her family know we're sorry."

"She doesn't even know that many people," I said. "She's very shy and they haven't lived here very long. Poor, poor Raisa."

All of the awful feelings I had when PJ died came back. It was different though; this time I didn't feel them for me, I felt them for Raisa. The phone rang and my Mom went to answer it.

"That was Mrs. Harrison," Mom said. "She was worried about you and wanted to make sure you got home all right. I told her you were here, and I asked her for Raisa's last name, address and phone number."

"Her name is Raisa Mehta," I said. "I guess I never told you her last name. I never asked her for her address or phone number."

"Do you think you'll be able to talk to Raisa if I call her home?" Mom asked.

I remembered how much it meant to me when Dan and Justin called to tell me they were sorry about PJ, and I nodded.

Mom went to the phone. I heard her introduce herself and say how sorry she was to hear about the death in their family. She asked if I could talk to Raisa. Mom thanked whoever she was talking to and handed me the phone.

"Raisa, I'm so sorry that your grandfather died. My best friend died last summer and I know how awful I felt then. I am so sorry for your sadness."

Raisa was quiet for a few minutes, I think she was trying not to cry, "I am surprised, but very glad, that you called," she said. "Thank you for caring about my sadness."

When Mr. Levine died, we brought cake. When PJ died, people sent flowers. I asked Raisa if Mom and I could get anything for her.

"No, thank you, but we will be home for "Kriya," which is our thirteen days of mourning," she told me. "You can come and visit if you'd like."

I asked my mom. She said to tell Raisa that we would stop at her house that night after my dad got home.

I told Raisa we'd visit later. She replied, "I'll be glad to see you. Thank you for being my friend."

When Dad got home, Mom and I told him about Raisa's grandfather. We ate a quick dinner and left for the Mehta's house.

There were a lot of people at the house when we arrived. Raisa's family greeted us and were very grateful that we'd come. I introduced Raisa to my parents and she explained that the Pandit, or Hindu priest, had just finished offering prayers for the spirit of her grandfather.

"All Hindus have a little Shrine or Temple in their homes but sometimes we *do* worship together in a bigger Temple. The Pandit comes from the big Temple," she said. Raisa's eyes were all red and puffy. I knew she'd been crying.

Most of the people were leaving and I asked Raisa why she and most of the others from India had white clothes on. She told me it was a Hindu custom to wear white when somebody died. I remembered how the priest had worn white at PJ's funeral.

My parents went over to talk with the Mehtas. Raisa and I sat down at the table in the kitchen. "What happened to your grandfather?" I asked.

"I don't really know," she answered. "He fell and hit his head. Later that night, he started throwing up and my father brought him to the hospital. He never came home."

I told her about PJ and his accident. I told her how much the "missing" hurt. I even told Raisa what Mom had said to me, "It'll take time for your bruised spirit to heal."

"Yes, you are right," she said. "I feel sorry for my grandmother, too. She and my grandfather were married for a very long time. It is so sad to see her missing him."

Just then, my parents came into the kitchen. They told me it was time to leave, but said that I could come back to see Raisa over the weekend.

"I'll be back and we can talk some more," I told her as we said good night.

On the way home, Mom and Dad told me that the Hindu custom is to cremate, or burn, the bodies of the dead. They believe that God made our bodies from the mud of the earth and that after we die our bodies should go back to the mud of the earth.

"That's not so different from the Bible," I said. "In First Day School, we read that God made our bodies from the soil."

"Right," Dad continued. "There is a river in India called the 'Ganges', which is holy to all Hindus. Whenever possible, the ashes left after the cremation are sprinkled on the River Ganges. That way the body returns to the mud on the bottom."

"Was Raisa's grandfather cremated?" I asked.

"Yes," said Mom. "Her parents told us tonight that his ashes are at the funeral home. Mr. Mehta will take his mother home to India to sprinkle them on the holy river."

That weekend I visited Raisa and we talked about a lot of things. I tried to remember everything my Grandma Peg had taught me so I could share it with her.

On Monday, when Raisa returned to school, I made sure she didn't have lunch alone and that we got a chance to work together.

It's strange. PJ's death, and the awful hurt I felt helped me to understand how Raisa felt.

CHAPTER 20

We had a lot of snow that January, and Matt and I had a chance to really "break in" his new sled. I even asked Justin and Dan to go with us a few times and we all had fun.

My birthday was coming soon—it's on February 18. Mom was getting bigger and bigger with the baby and was a little too tired to have a party. Dad said I could pick four friends and he would take us all bowling. I didn't know about asking Raisa, because she's a girl. Matt, Dan and Justin had already said they would love to go.

The week before my birthday I decided I didn't care that Raisa was a girl, she's my friend. I invited her to go bowling with us and she said yes.

Dad took us to the bowling alley, bought us lunch, and we all had to rent bowling shoes. None of us had ever bowled before so we were pretty funny. We laughed a lot, then dad took us home and mom had cake and ice cream ready for us. I got some real neat presents, both Grandma Peg and my Nana from Florida called, and it was a good birthday.

The next two months, March and April, went by really fast. Everything for the baby was ready, all the snow had melted, and things were beginning to grow again.

At the end of April, we had a bad thunderstorm with lots of lightning. One of the bolts of lightning hit the big old oak tree in PJ's back yard. I went to watch as the tree was cut down and chopped into small pieces. The men put the pieces into a very loud machine called a chipper. When they'd finished, there was nothing left of the tree. I never liked the tree after PJ's accident and was glad it was gone.

Grandma Peg was at our house because it was almost time for the baby. I brought Raisa home to meet her, and Grandma Peg asked Raisa all about London and India. When it was time for Raisa to leave, Mom and Grandma Peg invited her to come back, and to bring her grandmother with her.

Raisa said her grandmother was still very sad about her grandfather's death but that she really liked little babies. "Maybe when your new baby comes I can get her to come over to see the baby."

That sounded like a good idea. "Now we just have to wait for the baby," I said.

I didn't have to wait long. About a week later, I woke up in the middle of the night and heard voices. Dad came into my room and said it was time to take Mom to the hospital. I went downstairs, gave my mom a hug, and stood at the door with Grandma Peg as my parents left. The baby was on the way!

"How long does it take for a baby to be born?" I asked my grandma.

"Babies come when they get good and ready," she answered. "Let's have some milk and cookies and try to get some more sleep. Your dad will call us as soon as the baby comes. We'll probably hear from him sometime tomorrow."

"Tomorrow? It takes that long?" I moaned.

"Being born is hard work," Grandma said. "Don't rush your new brother or sister. It'll happen soon enough."

We had our snack and went back to bed. When it was time to get up, I didn't want to go to school. I was afraid I'd miss Dad's phone call. Grandma Peg said we didn't have a new baby every day and that I could stay home.

The morning seemed so long that day. Grandma Peg had just made soup for lunch when the phone rang. She told me I could answer it and I ran to pick it up.

"Hello," I said.

"You have a new baby sister!" I heard my dad say. "Mom and the baby are fine and you and Grandma can come to see them both at four o'clock."

"Yippee!" I shouted. "Grandma Peg, it's a girl!"

My grandmother got on the phone and talked to my dad. He told her he'd call Nana in Florida. Grandma asked him if he'd had anything to eat and told him we'd meet him at the hospital that afternoon.

I was really glad the baby was a girl, because my mom, dad and I had a secret. We had planned to surprise both my grandmothers and name the baby, if it was a girl, after both of them.

Grandma Peg's real name is Margaret. Peg is a nickname for Margaret. My Nana's name is Anne. The baby's name would be Margaret Anne. We'd call her "Meg," which is another nickname for Margaret. I couldn't wait for my grandmothers to find out!

We got to the hospital at ten minutes to four. Dad was waiting for us, hugged us both, and told us that the baby was beautiful. He took us up to my Mom's room and we went in.

"Hi, big brother," Mom said. "Come see your new baby sister."

The baby was in a little crib next to my mom's bed. She had soft, curly hair and her little hands were perfect. She was wide awake and just looking around at everything.

"Wow, she's tiny. Do you think she knows I'm here?" I asked.

"Sure she does," Mom said, "and so do I. Where's my hug?"

I gave her a hug, "Sorry, Mom. The baby's amazing and I got distracted."

"She sure is!" said Grandma Peg. "What a lovely little girl."

Dad said, "Let's call Nana in Florida. That way we can all say hello."

I knew that it was time to tell them the baby's name. I got all excited as Dad got my Nana on the phone. He told her we were all there and even let me tell her how pretty the baby was. Then Mom took the phone.

"We wanted to tell you both at once. Nana and Grandma Peg, the baby's name is Margaret Anne, after both of you," Mom told them. "We'll call her Meg."

Grandma Peg started crying, I guess Nana did, too. My grandmothers talked to each other on the phone and Mom, Dad and I felt pretty good about our secret. The baby had a name!

I guess we were making too much noise, because little Meg started to cry. Dad picked her up and made quiet little noises while he rocked her back and forth. The baby stopped crying and snuggled in my dad's arms.

"Tomorrow, you can sit in that big chair and you can hold her," Mom said as she looked at me.

"Me? I don't know. She's so little."

"She'll snuggle up with you, too," Dad said. "Babies know when they're loved."

CHAPTER 21

We stayed a little while longer, then Dad said both Mom and Meg needed to rest. I kissed Mom good-bye, touched the baby's hand, and Dad, Grandma Peg and I went home.

The next day at school, I told everyone about Meg. I told the whole class about surprising my grandmothers, too.

Raisa said she knew when I'd been out the day before that the baby had come. She gave me a little hat called a bonnet that her grandmother had made for Meg. It was very small and had lace, ribbons and little colored flowers on it.

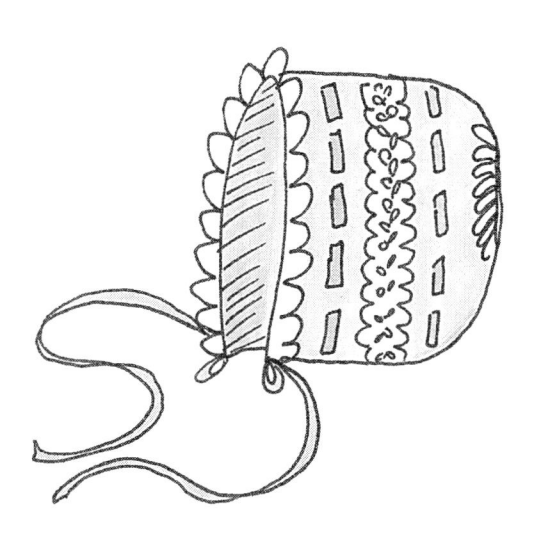

"Tell your grandmother, 'Thanks'. It was really nice of her to make this for the baby," I told Raisa. " Now she *has* to come and see Meg."

When Mom and the baby came home, Grandma Peg took care of things so Mom could rest. Dad went back to work, I went to school, and except for Meg keeping us up a few nights, things in our house settled down.

Meg grew every day and I loved to watch her discover new things. After a while, she'd laugh when I talked to her and made silly faces. Mrs. Olson brought the twins over to see her and they got all excited about "the baby." It's funny, before Meg, I'd always thought of Ellen and Elizabeth as babies.

Raisa brought her grandmother to our house to see Meg, and while the grownups talked I took Raisa to see my "secret" pond in the park. Matt and the other guys came to see the baby, too. Dan's mom was going to have a baby in a few months so he was really curious.

School was almost over, Grandma Peg was getting ready to go back to the farm, and summer was on the way. There were two more weeks of school and I couldn't wait for vacation to start!

Dad said, "Last year, you asked your grandmother about going to the farm for the whole summer. Mom will be home with Meg so you don't have to go to day camp if you don't go to the farm. What would *you* like to do? It's your choice."

Last summer there had been no Meg, and PJ had just died. I loved the farm and Grandma Peg, but I didn't know if I wanted to be away from Meg that long. She was changing so fast, I didn't want to miss it all.

Grandma Peg came to my rescue, "If I stay until school gets out, you can come to the farm with me. In three weeks, we'll come back here, so I can check on my new granddaughter. You can decide then, what you want to do for the rest of the summer."

"Great idea, Grandma. You've been here helping us, so things at the farm must need some work. I'll help you and then decide.

CHAPTER 22

I stayed home when Grandma Peg brought me back. We'd had a great time at the farm, but Meg was growing, Matt and Raisa were around, and I just wanted to be home for a while. Grandma Peg understood.

In July, on the first anniversary of PJ's death, my whole family, even Meg, went to Church with the Gonzales family. There was a Mass in memory of PJ and Mrs. Gonzales had asked us to go. I thought about the last time I'd been in Saint Francis Church and how awful I'd felt. Time had helped me to heal.

Mom, Dad and I did some fun things, too. We had picnics, went to the beach, and even took Meg along a couple of times. The summer went by so fast!

September came way too soon. This year I have my first man teacher, Mr. Curtis, and still play with Matt, Raisa, Justin and Dan. Dan's mom had a baby boy. They named him Joseph.

We're getting ready for Thanksgiving now. This year the Gonzales family *is* coming, and so are the Mehtas. Miss Sherman's coming back, the Kings from Meeting are coming, and, of course, Grandma Peg. There'll be eighteen people at our house this year for Meg's first Thanksgiving.

It's been almost a year and a half now since PJ died. I still think of him, and all of the fun we used to have. Mom was right. It doesn't hurt as much now as it did that summer...but I'll never forget PJ. I'll always remember him as the best friend any kid could ever have.

It's almost my birthday, and I *do* have new friends. Matt, Raisa, and my new baby sister, Meg, have taught me lots. I guess the most important things I've learned since PJ died are that *everyone* hurts when they lose someone they care about, and as Grandma Peg says, "If you're worrying about dying, you're messing up your *living*."

One thing hasn't changed though. I still hate strawberry jam. I don't think I'll *ever* like strawberry jam again—even when I'm all grown up! Mom and Dad say that's OK.

GLOSSARY

bruised

    an injury when the skin turns black and blue.

casket

    a box, usually small; word often used when referring to a coffin.

cemetery

    a place where dead people are buried; a graveyard.

ceremony

    a formal act, or set of acts, determined by ritual or custom.

choir loft

    the upstairs balcony used by an organized group of singers, usually in a church.

coffin

    a box in which a dead body is buried.

cremation
>to burn a dead body into ashes.

drill bits
>the metal tips of a tool used to drill holes.

First Day School
>the Quaker religion classes, held on Sunday, for both children and adults.

4H
>a national organization, started in 1902, to enable young people from Kindergarten to age 19 to pick their own projects and learn by doing. The symbol is a four leaf clover with an H on each leaf, standing for Head, Heart, Hands, Health.

funeral
>the ceremonies held with the burial or cremation of the dead.

Funeral Director
    a professional trained to prepare bodies after death and to assist families in planning a funeral and burial or cremation.

funeral home
    the building where the Funeral Director works and where the body is kept until burial or cremation. It is also where a wake or viewing is held.

Funeral Mass
    a Catholic ceremony, held in a church, with prayers for the person who is dead and prayers for all their family and friends.

grave
    a place where a dead body is buried.

grieving
    feeling deep sadness over a loss; sorrow.

harvest
    the gathering of a crop.

Hindu
> a religion, started in India over five thousand years ago. Hindus believe that Brahman (God) can show himself or herself in many forms.

incense
> a substance burned to produce a pleasant odor.

Kriya
> for Hindus, the thirteen days of mourning after a person dies.

Mass
> for Catholics, the celebration of Jesus' death and resurrection.

Meeting for Worship
> the Quaker way of worship, meeting together to listen and speak to God and one another.

mourning
> feeling sorrow or grief.

Native Peoples
>in each country, the people who were the first inhabitants are called the "natives." When Columbus landed in the North America, he thought he was in India and called the people here "Indians." There were many different tribes and we know now that these were the "native peoples" of this country.

Pandit
>the Hindu leader of prayer.

pregnant
>expecting a baby.

priest
>one who is selected by God, and blessed (ordained) by a specific religious group, to preach, lead others in prayer and worship, and give the sacraments if the particular religion uses outward signs to show God's love and support.

Rabbi
> originally "teacher," now the ordained spiritual leader of a Jewish congregation.

ritual
> an act or set of acts determined by a specific group of people to express a belief they share.

Shiva
> in Hebrew, the language of the Jews, it means seven, also the seven days of mourning following the burial of the dead. In Hindi, the language of Hindus, if is the name of one of the many forms God takes.

Shiva call
> a visit to a Jewish house, during the seven days following burial, when people are mourning for someone who died.

stethoscope
> an instrument used to listen to sounds within the body.

Sunday School
>religious classes held on a Sunday, for both children and adults.

sympathy
>feeling or expression of sorrow over the sadness or loss of another.

Synagogue
>Jewish House of Worship.

Temple
>can be used to describe a Hindu, Jewish or Muslim House of Worship.

viewing
>a visit to a funeral home, usually when the dead person can be seen lying in the coffin, to express sympathy to the grieving family.

wake
>an older term, meaning to keep watch over, now used the same way as "viewing."